HOME ON THE UPPER EAST SIDE

David Lawrence

ISBN: 978-81-19228-63-8

First Edition: 2023
Rs. 200/-

Cyberwit.net
HIG 45 Kaushambi Kunj, Kalindipuram
Allahabad - 211011 (U.P.) India
http://www.cyberwit.net
Tel: +(91) 9415091004
E-mail: info@cyberwit.net

Printed at Repro India Limited.

Contents

So Many

I have almost no income but I live on the upper east side with rich people who wash their brains in soda water and pop, pop, pop goes their details and minutiae. They go to work. They come home. They shop. They slop around in the creases of their small brains and boast their minks like stupid slaughters. They dedicate themselves to goods but they are not good because their brains are small and tiny is as tiny does. Bezos hitches a ride to space and doesn't realize that he is out of it, that he is a mistake in a rash of details, that he is a false integer. Money is not integrity. It is an excuse for failed appreciation of the beautiful. When I was in the business world the business of the world was choking me and I spit out teeth like chicklets. My brain was as numb as my gums and I didn't understand what I didn't understand because I was lost in blank scrabble tiles. "Death be not proud." What does that have to do with anything? Words come to me like foreign ideas in unrecognizable languages. I am assaulted by impulses. I want to punch people in the faces as I walk down the street. But I don't. That is another person talking. I hardly hear it. It is the voice of dissociated personalities. I can control my behavior but not my thoughts. I am so many, so many. A crowd lives inside of me. I wish I could identify with the loneliest identity.

Coffee Cart

I walk over to the coffee cart at 71st and Park.
There are a few construction workers
On line.
Could I beat them up?
Could they be mine?
George Harrison sang, "All through the day/
I me mine, I me mine, I me mine/
All through the night/
I me mine, I me mine, I me mine."

What are these slobs doing online on the upper east side?
Constructing?
Erecting?
Intellectual vegetating?

But I don't start in.
I just pull my shoulders back so I look a little bit taller.
But that exposes my face.
In boxing I put my head down so that I could slip punches.
It works.
Sometimes.
Four broken noses are technical errors.

Three dollars.
Not bad for a vanilla donut,
A large coffee
And an egg.
Not as good as the cart at 74th and Lexington where I get

Three Gatorades,
Two eggs,
A pink donut
And a large coffee for seven dollars.

I worry about cart prices.
I used to order caviar and champagne at Le Cirque.
Life is up and down.
I am the clown who is juggling with his down phase.
It started in jail.
When I am manic I ride the whale of superior feelings.
Jonah don't let me down,
Don't let me drown.
Sound is not sound but orchestral confidence.
It's all in the Gatorade.
That is the cost.
That is the good buy.
Seven dollars is as seven dollars does.
It buys me a whole bad of goodies.

The wizard in the cart at Lexington Avenue is behind panels.
He is an Arab.
One of my favorite movies is *Lawrence of Arabia.*
I saw it in London.
I was eighteen.
I was with my girlfriend's older brother.
He was a Harvard snob.
I didn't like him.
I wanted to die on a camel bleached by the sun.
As long as he wasn't near me like an intellectual scorpion
In the Sahara.

Harvard was what it was when it was.
The fall of an academic empire.
Now Nero is fiddling
In the political science department with his woke
Instrument.

My Neighborhood

I am in my neighborhood or my neighborhood is in me
And lifts me by the scruff of my neck
Like a cat pawing the upper classes.

I live on Park and Seventy-Second Street.
I no longer belong here.
I don't have a job.
I love teaching boxing but it is not a career.
Poet?
I can't earn a dime even though I have published
Sixteen books.
I am living on borrowed time in a plentiful
Bank of stuffiness.

If I hate the rich, I must hate my past.
So be it.
Continuity is a fear of change.
I look forward to whatever come what may.

I walk down the block to the grocery store.
So I ad lib on Pearl Jam:
"Oh where oh where has my Rolls Royce gone?"
The Lord took her away from me
She's gone to heaven, so I got to be good
So I can see my baby when I leave this world.
Or so I can get a lift when I leave this world.

Pearl Jam was singing about a girl not a Rolls Royce,
F..K the girl.

Try returning a leased Rolls to the dealer when
You still have two years to run on the lease.
The dealer understood when I told him
That I was going to jail
I'm freezing.
I don't belong in the artic circle of wasted funds.
I pick up a sandwich
And Gator-Aid.
I am happy.

I am gay.
Not gay.
Happy.
You know what I mean even though you are not reading me.
My books are not too popular.
Genius is misunderstood and ignored.

Woke society's failure is an inability to be honest
About what it feels.
Judgmental is the failure of small minds.
Liberal is the restrictive authoritarian
Views of the pretend humanitarians.

I am not seeing any passerby's but I imagine a face
I want to punch and a body I want to break.
Do I want to knife him?
That would be fun.
It wouldn't.

Why do I tease myself with pretend acts where I have no intention.
In high school I had permanent detention.
I graduated to jail.
I was nailed by the taxman and now have to read by braille.

I buy what I buy and leave my gloves in my pocket
So that my hands hurt from the sub-freezing weather.
Ow. Pain is lovely.
I like it.
I am a masochist.
I want to show that I can be strong and take it.

I think of poking my eyes out.
I don't mean it.
I mean that I am crazy and think what I don't think
To prove that I am insane.
I am not.
I am a pain in the normal psyche.
I try to hold it all together as my brain is falling apart.
When the little pieces hit the floor they wiggle.
I giggle at my predicament on the cement.
They are worms.
They are thoughts.
They are tackle to arouse the love mouths of fish.

I Just Don't Care

I walk east on 74th Street to the food cart. Rich I am. Or was. Now I dine on donuts and coffee. Not wine. Well, I never drank wine in the morning. I don't remember the labels at the four-star restaurants. Trump calls the fake news fake. It is. It isn't. Labeling it such doesn't do much for identity. It undercuts reality with bitterness. America is going through an identity crisis. It is identifying with identity rather than emotional retrieval. The man who owns the cart is an Arab. I liked Arabs when I was in Tunisia. When they knocked our buildings into Ground Zero, I hated them. I like the coffee man because he sells me coffee and sundries like eggs, donuts and Gatorade. I love Gatorade. I would f..k it if I could. I shouldn't joke like that. Why not? F..k you, I am what I am and I am not Popeye the Sailor Man but rich Joey Brown on his yacht in "Some Like It Hot." If I were Marilyn Monroe, I would finger myself. I'd probably do it better than Joe DiMaggio. You are gross. I'm gross. The whole world is gross and I am phat with degenerate beats. I put a sign on my forehead, "Children beware." Not of me but my words. My morals are threadbare. I say what I say. Beware. I just don't care.

Seventy-Second Street

When I get used to something I get used to it and become
familiar
With the Upper East Side.
I lost my job.
I went to jail.
If I can find a way to still live here
I will die here.
They can bury me on Park Avenue in Prada.
Maybe a philanthropist will rent me a space
In the window.
He can put me in a tux in a lacquered open coffin.
Passerby's will say that handsome is as handsome does
Even when I am dead.
As James Dead said,
"Live fast, die young, leave a good-looking corpse."
Who am I kidding?
I am seventy-four.
I missed my chance to die young.
I guess there is something to living that appeals to me.
Maybe I like Seventy-Second Street.
I am comfortable like five stairs in front of a brownstone.
I want to snuggle up in the prewar buildings.
The women are old.
The men are old.
The dogs are old.
I am old and fit into my neighborhood like I am putting
On an old coat.
It would be wrong for a mugger to come around here.
It wouldn't be right for him to crack

On a population of old porcelain vases.
He'd be surprised if he started in with me.
He would end his life with his initiation.
He would join the fraternity of the dead.
I'd like to kill him.
Manliness is what has shrunken from modern society
And transgenderism is the dead mind
Losing its balls.
I do not forgive Bruce Jenner for becoming a woman.
If you transform into a vagina
You should sing in falsetto
Because you are a false transformation into not-ness
Like a misguided barren planet.
You consider me opinionated.
It is better than not having the courage to have opinions
At all.

The Monster on The Upper East Side

I am the monster on the upper east side.
Not really.
I am a nice guy.
Oh, so nice.
I would throw rice at your wedding and wish
You the best.

I'd buy you a present and not even borrow
The money.
I am giving.
Sadly, my past has given too much of me away.
I was careless.
Not that I didn't care.
I just didn't notice.
I was a blind man without a cane.

Only my thoughts have scales and fire breath,
Death.
I want to kill everyone who
Passes me by on Park Avenue.
I am the thought
That never meets up with its result.
My thoughts are not even mine.
They are someone else's.
The footnotes of chemical engineering,
Life's test tubes.

I am the anger that dissipates like ginger ale.
My ideas have nothing to do with me.

I don't really rape little girls
Or poodles.
I don't punch old men in the nose
Or say " my nigger."
I am not a white liberal camouflaged in the emotional
Black face of BLM.

I am a do nothing.
I am the fantasy of violence in a Ralph Lauren
Storefront window.
But I have the disposition of a little old lady knitting.
My life is a sweater.
I put it on and imagine violence in the threads.

Don't worry if you hate me.
I have the same feeling too even if I don't mean it
And don't know what I mean.

Uptown Girl

I am sitting in my bedroom in my multimillion-dollar coop and reflecting that I only earn forty dollars an hour for boxing lessons. How does this compute? I am the contraction that keeps contradicting itself but never smashes on the edges of different directions. I am here, there, everywhere. I am this and that and phat like a fat MC's beats. I was on TV with Fat Joe. Call me skinny Dave. Billy Joel loved his, *Uptown girl/ She's been living in her uptown world/ I bet she's never had a backstreet guy/ I bet her momma never told her why.* Sigh. Sigh. Sigh. I am living in both the uptown world and I have become a backstreet guy. I belong in the bowery. I cherish the sky. I did two years fed time. I was happier there than here. You have to fall to rise spiritually. God has blood on his palms. I am his son, the Sun and the radiance of completion. One day they will write a bible about me. They already have. Christ is not jealous. He lets me identify with him but will not suffer my praise or prayers.

The Boston Strangler

Albert DeSalvo didn't live on the Upper East Side.
Abide by what you abide
But don't lie to yourself about who you are.

He was so divided that he didn't know
One from the other.
I am not divided.
My personality is not split.
I am the fog that covers personalities.
I am neither here nor there and recognize
The in between.

I am capable of anything because I am nothing.
I am me and you and you
Without much ado
But nothing dramatic like a murder drama.

I am David and David and David.
We are all the same but different and tend towards the insane
While we know exactly what we are doing
And who we are.

The killer in me is a noblesse oblige king.
He is a bum sleeping under a blanket at the doorway to Prada.
I would never strangle a woman.
I am afraid that I might but I am afraid of everything that I am not.
I don't know me.
I am glad to meet me.

No, I am not because if I am what I accuse myself of being than
I would rather not be.
Do you have any idea what it is like to be me?

I don't know who I am and identification is a mindless opinion.
The dead women remain nameless.

Albert DeSalvo becomes the protagonist of his own story
And morphs in the movie into Tony Curtis.
Tony is too good looking for a murderer.
Sins are painted on our faces in the attic like "The Picture of
Dorian Gray."
George Sanders was spared.
His portrait told the story without the necessity of the strangula-
tions.
The paints had a life of their own.
Murder can be colorful and smudged like hurt feelings and faces.

Back to the Boston Strangler.
The movie scared me.
I am worried that my personality is split when I know that it is
not
Split but comes hither and thither like powerful hands.
I strangle you.
I strangle me.
I am choking the life out of death so that I can compromise
And become guilt free like a goldfish out of his bowl on the
kitchen floor.

Filthy Me

I am a divided country.
You are a c..t tree.
That's a gratuitous curse.
That language says a lot about what
I say but don't mean,
A scream is a scream is a scream.

You are disgusting.
I am disgusting.
We all are disgusting,
Especially the virtue signaling.

I yell at my crude language.
A c..t is a nude shrub.
Women hate that word.
F..k em.
If only I could.
I hate women.
I love them.
I am words floating in the sky,
Meaning nothing.
My oh my I am the space bouncing between
Ideas like a pogo stick.

I look at myself in the invisible mirror
And see the resemblance to my face
Which is erased but there.
Trying to know myself is a reflection
Of sincere introspection.

Come back to me as a personal identity.
I am not black,
White,
Yellow,
Or red.

I am what happens at the center of color,
The meaning of meaning.
I am illustrious.
I am David,
A sincere confusion.

Hide your wife.
I'm only playing.
I am the joker,
A powerhouse in a hand of cards.
I think.
The Joker is another suit.
Ask Joachim Phoenix.
I don't remember.
I remember that I don't remember.
I know that he was sick.
I sense it in my smile when he smiles at me.

F..k Tribeca

They say that Tribeca has become ritzier than the upper east side. I once saw John John Kennedy walking down Franklin Street. I was going to my poetry seminar at Jill Hoffman's. The next year he died in a stupid airplane crash. He should have taken the warning of his dad's fate. It is too late and Tribeca makes its bid for priority when it is mired in its dark, mediocre past. Give me Park Avenue and Fifth in the sixties, seventies and eighties. F..k Tribeca. Let me make love to the Upper East Side. I live at 74th and Park. Let me lie down naked beneath an autumn sky and f..k the sidewalk. I belong here. I can reproduce my image through my thighs under the sky. I don't want women to walk on the small of my back near Park. I want my wife to lift me by the neck and to put a wet hanky on my forehead and tell me that I am not the division between five personalities but that I am the love of her life when my life is flattened into postures that can't defend themselves.

Insane Dancing

There is a book "The War Without the Mind" which mistakenly tells you that you should fight a bipolar condition. Bad advice. When you fight a warrior you become a victim of the edge of his sword. Gladiators die early deaths. Better to dance with your fate and be a cloud in a failed storm. I give in to my mania. I give in to my depression. Giving in turns antagonism into solipsism. I become the introspective result of dodging bullets in a vest. John Poehler puts a boxing glove and heavy bag on the cover of his book. He was never a fighter. He is not rich like me. Neither am I. I lost my business in 1993. That set me free from pecuniary responsibilities. I think. Poehler seems like a good guy but his advice stinks. Fred Astaire and Ginger Rogers do the trick. You must dance with your insanity if you want to end up in formal dress at a swank party. I don't walk on water. I walk on Fifth Avenue alongside Central Park. I confuse myself with God. Then I watch a bum shit on the corner. I don't want to help him. I have my own problems.

Not So

I want to hit you over the head with a baseball bat.
The brains fall in.
The brains fall out.
They crawl all over your dirty snout….

I want to play with your brains like dough.
I don't mean it.
I am a killer.
I am a thriller.
I like to pass the time with morbid thoughts.

I have lived in a top upper east side apartment
And in jail.
I can't tell the difference.
I am a bunk bed.
I am a marble floor in front of a mantel piece
Where I used to sleep when my wife kicked me out of the bedroom.

Jesse Waters said on television that if you think it
You might do it.
He has a good job.
He is a moron.
He rode nasty O'Reilly's coat tails.
If I did everything I imagined I would have been
Executed a thousand times.
I would have deserved it.

Thinking it doesn't make it so.
I am not various and split personalities but I am the

Rubber raft that floats over the different shapes
And colors of jellyfish.
I do not live in the slums.
Circumstances have taken away my money.

My thoughts still pile up inside of me like Fort Knox.
It's not that I am innocent.
It's that all the rest of you are guilty too.
Getting caught is getting even with the ups and downs of societal norms.

It was just tax evasion.
Now virtue signaling attorney generals
Are letting people go free for smash and grab,
Car jackings and violent crimes.
And will they let the rapists of their daughters free?

It fits the paradigm.
The liberals turn the world upside down as they misinterpret crime.
The real crime is forgiving the criminals.
If you don't have values
You don't have values and the world is a wasteland
Of ashen codes.

I pinch hit for real criminals when I launder money on a backyard Clothesline.

I am nothing.
I am the crime that never arrived at violence.
I pick myself up by the white collar like a cat by the scruff of his neck.

Petula Clark Sings "Downtown"

She did. Way back then. I don't hear it now. I do. In my head.
She sang, "When you're alone and life is making you lonely
You can always go
Downtown."
F..k that.
I am an uptown boy from the Upper East Side
Where rich is rich and I was rich but have fallen from grace,
Not gracefully,
But I took my jail sentence like a man.
I still have my manners.
I still knit grace into grace and wave the handkerchief of my persona
With the linen
Of money that I no longer have.
I hate downtown.
I live where I live because I am who I am even though
I am no longer a rich man but I maintain my grace and charm.
Who am I kidding?
My class trails behind me like a case of mistaken identity.
John Lennon sang, *I'm a loser/I'm a loser/And I'm not what I appear to be.*
Petula Clark sang on John Lennon's "Give Peace a Chance."
Liberals are too soft.
Peace didn't give John a chance.
If Chapman had been in a mental institution, he wouldn't have killed John.
If John had been armed, he would still be writing songs.
I would carry a gun but I don't want to shoot myself.
I am a threat.
I am not.

Oh, I don't know.
I imagine.
I am confused.
And the underbelly of downtown is the disruption of propriety.
I am proud to wear the upper east side like a crown.
If you want to pay more for a coop downtown then you are throwing
Money down a sewer that is all decked up with the flowers of persuasion
And the hypocrisy of making something out of nothing.
Reverse snobbery is still bigotry.
The definition of downtown is a downer.
Living offbeat does not put you on the beat and Soho
Is a failure to strut like a gentleman on Park Avenue.
Give me class.
I am not a Bentley that pretends that it is humble by taking
The Winged Victory off of the hood.
You can't hide.
You are what you are.
And me?
I am no longer what I be but I have the exhaust pipe of failure.
You think that living downtown you are superior to uptown
Because you are on the downlow.
It's all a competitive game.
You lose.
I win.
I am the broke person on Park Avenue and 74th Street.
But I am not broken.
I am David come back from the dead to reincarnate optimism.

A Casual Breath in A Vase

If you are bipolar you flip from extreme to extreme like an acrobat.
The upper east side doesn't play around on the trapeze.
It is staid.
It is for played out money and careless suits.
It is formal while it is casual and laissez faire without the impetus
To dare to take risks.

Tsk. Tsk. It is right where you would want it if you wanted stasis
And the consistency of not having to care about getting
Mugged by a teenager.
It is a girdle not panties.

It is a casual breath in a vase and a rose by the name of class.

So when you tell me that I should move downtown to an eight
Million dollar coop I say I would rather live uptown where
Real is real
Than downtown where artistic is autistic confusion.

I haven't lost my mind.

I teach autistic children boxing on Saturdays at Gleason's Gym.
Some kids are repetitive.
Some are remote.
Some are anti-social.

I know what they mean. I know what they mean.

I am part of their dream and they have entered mine.
I am streaming on someone else's channel.
I am lost in their lostness.

I am the upper east side.
Not it's glitz,
Not its pomp and circumstance,
Just its calm identity as a piece of a prewar building,
A part of the façade of this poem.
I am not polished stone.
I am the occasional senior citizen who wanders aimlessly
About the East Seventies
Forgetting where his home is as he returns from
Gleason's Gym where he just sparred six rounds like
He was still a pro.

I am a unique case.
You can check out my record at Mt. Sinai Hospital.
It's not bad.
I have seen the neurologist, the psychiatrist and the psychologist.
Tests?
What do I know?
I am trying to find the peace in the extremes.
I am almost sprinting in a tight mental cage.

You Will Get Burnt

Seventy-second Street is a two-way street. I go in twenty directions. I am inflated, bifurcated, at least. They say that living in the neighborhood I should be sedate and calm as a turtle's shell. I would not want to be an ugly snail crawling around the East Seventies. I do not want to be a snapping turtle like my neighbor who bites at the doorman and holds his stupid position as the ridiculous chairman of a joke board above the other tenants. I am a gentleman. Always was. Always will be. Even though I am a professional boxer and spent two years in jail. That doesn't affect me. I am class. I am above the disaffections that fate has foisted upon me with accidental failures. From an outside perspective I don't belong here. From the inside I am the soul of the uptown city where I keep the rain of self-pity from my shoulders like a self-confident raincoat. I am proud. Not gay pride but pride for my Ph.D., my publications, my earlier fortune, my athletic rankings, my rap and jazz albums, my movies, my being me. Look the other way. You are so busy playing the role of uptown that you can't see that I am the buildings that dwarf you. I am edifice. I am stone. You are the gentleman who has forgotten how to be gentle and stomps on weaklings as if you are stepping on cigars. One day your shoes won't be there. You will get burnt.

Sub Zero

1
A few afternoons ago my Sub Zero refrigerator sprung a leak.
What am I doing with a Sub Zero?
I am a down and out boxing trainer who once was rich,
La de la de da,
But now I am poor,
Becoming the landed gentry living in a multi-million-dollar coop
Without the cash of a cash cow.

I suppose I am aristocratic.
We have had some experience with repairman before.
Aaron had left a sticker on our refrigerator.
It's a cold wind that blows when
I get stuck with repair bills from my past lifestyle.
He sent an Hispanic kid to do the work.
I love Hispanics.
I hate them because the only two times I was knocked out in boxing
Were from Hispanics.
I don't remember his name.
Was it Manuel?
Enchilada?
Tortilla?
I didn't take him through our living room
Because I didn't want him to see all of the antiques.
Maybe he was a thief.
That is a cliché.
He's after my hubcaps.
But cliches are repetitive truths.

He visits my apartment and mistakes me for one
Of the monied class,
Harassed by pressure
And trying to make it in the makeshift world.

Nice young guy.
I want to cry that I am not a working man.
Mechanics is a gift.
I want to work on the refrigerator on his shift.

I get along better with him than my accountant.
My accountant charges me integers
For all my zeros.

2
The plumber didn't take time for a siesta.
He changed the damaged part in twenty- minutes while my
porter mopped
The floor.

The bill was five hundred and fifty dollars.
If only I could trade my Ph.D. in for a plumbing certificate.
I didn't tip anyone.
I am not cheap.
I am poor.
He replaced this or that.
Ta da, done is done if it is really done.
Who knows?
I would if I could see the future wood.
Norwegian wood.
What does that have to do with anything?
The Beatles have fired up my memory.

I was a member of the American Boxing team that was sched-
uled
To fight the Norwegian Olympic team
But didn't.
Thank God.
Maybe.

3
Four days later there was a flood on my kitchen floor
That was worse than worse and could have drowned Noah.
No. Maybe. Who knows?
I am an hysteric.
I called our super at two in the morning and he drove in
From Lake Ronkonkoma.
He turned off the water in the line
And the flood receded.
We waited for the refrigerator repairman.
I was trying to decide whether I would stiff Aaron's repairman
For having to return
Because my current flood was his failure.
Where was eloquent Aaron when I needed him?

Imagine being Moses' brother.
Well, I am Christ's son.
That's not bad.
But I don't believe in self-sacrifice when I can punch
You in the mouth.
I hate myself for no reason.
It has nothing to do with your sins or mine.
I am hanging around on a cross waiting for the exuberance of
death.

4
The same refrigerator repair man shows up at the door.
I had misperceived him.
I thought he was an Hispanic mugger.
He was nice as spice if he were not harsh
Which he wasn't
At all.

We chatted like old friends.
I get along better with the lower classes because I
Am under the snobbish rain clouds,
All wet with friendliness.
I don't like the rich.
Let me roll in the crumbs with the kitchen rodents.
This is no insult to the poor.
My insults point up not down.
I dislike my betters because they are not really better.

His name is Mike.
Mine is David.
The exchange of names is the handshake of almost friendship.
It's a cold wind that blows inside the Sub Zero.
Not so bad outside the broken ice maker.

5
The last time I got a bill for his work which is something something
And I can no longer peak at the refrigerator's
Leak.

He had charged me five hundred and fifty dollars.
For the upper east side that's cheap.

He's not a creep.
I swear it.

He gets what he can get because getting is possession
And possession is nine tenths of the law.

This time it is no charge.
I fall down in a swoon of happiness and kiss his cuffs.
I don't.
But I feel that good.

I crack jokes.
I don't remember them.

I tell him that I teach boxing
Not to threaten him but because I am proud
Not of money
But of being a man in a genderless land where mental
Illness has no sex organs.
Nice guy.
I cry.
Because I like to do opposite of what I feel and tears dry
After they've said what they have said.

Prufrock Revisited

This morning I went out on 74th Street. Did I? I don't remember. Dementia is a street sign without a label. It keeps washing itself clean. I am directionless in wiped out names. I don't know where I am going. I am gone. At least, part way. I have approached the island of Alzheimer's and found beautiful women in bikinis rubbing my chemistry. When I look on the stoops, I can't find the steroids. I am a product of my test tubes. I went to my second favorite cart to get coffee and a donut but there was no cart. The owner must have been home sick. He might have had coronavirus. I don't give a shit. There is dog shit and a plastic glove on the corner. I must, I must, I must have coffee. I go to overpriced Ralph Lauren. I get a croissant, a coffee and a blueberry muffin for my wife. I go home. I look for my clock. I don't know where I put it. If you don't know the time you can't measure your thoughts. I am obsessed with the clock. I wake up every few hours to look at it. Prufrock is a dull tool who measured his life with coffee spoons. I am not a perfectionist. I have a sloppy sense of humor. I measure my life by what I dribble onto my shirt when I laugh.

Home

"Sitting at a railway station looking for my destination—
Home."
Paul Simon.
Big deal.
A little man.
I hated him.
I liked his songs even though they were folksy
Rather than rock and roll.

I heard he was nasty.
Perhaps a rumor.
Nastiness is a refuge for the fearful.
I wanted to knock him out.
He was rumored to box.
Not a big shot.
I was a pro.
He was about the size of Agapitos.
I sparred with Agapitos.
Simon would have been knocked before he stepped
In the ring.
Agapitos was shot in the Dominican Republic.
He was the champ.
It didn't stop the bullet.

I am on the F train again.
Going to Gleason's.
I used to make millions in insurance.
I was driven in a Rolls Royce
Not the F train.

I have a bit of dementia like chewing tobacco.
Is it because I am seventy-four,
That I went to jail
Or that I was hit thousands of times in the head?

I hated insurance.
I love boxing but I'm surely not a champ.
A champ is someone who sticks to what he is doing
Like a fly on orange paper
Who can't get out of his own way.

I am a failure.
I have written 16 books.
I was once the limousine of youth.
I rapped three albums.
I wrote a jazz LP.
I was ranked in skiing, tennis and boxing.

I have done a lot.
Not.
I stink.
I am a failure with a part time job as a boxing trainer.
I duck your punches.
I get hit in the temple.
I have dropped out at the spot where I went to jail.

All hail me.
The worms hail Jay.
"Men In Black" goes at the top of my stack.
I have had a full empty life.
I chew on failure like a cop eating
A donut in his car.
Police me down.

I am arrested by getting caught at doing nothing.
I wrote a book,
"This Book About Nothing."
It was really something.
Only, no one noticed.
I am hitch hiking on fame but no one picks me up.
I am not crying.
I am walking on the shoulder of the road.
I slap the bushes.
I am in touch with the ground.

Gay Pride

I am proud of living on the Upper East Side. The architecture and the buildings are so discrete. I eat in fastidious restaurants. I respect my rich elderly neighbors. I have no desire to hang out in mindless nooses with the lower east side young. I do not have counterculture gay pride. I am not gay. I am not a goy. I am Christ's son breaking away from his religion like he smashed the ten commandments. Oh, that was Moses. Who cares? I wrote a book, "God Is Me...Whoopee." It was never published. It will be. It was.

I am we and me is I. I am a poor boy in a rich neighborhood. I love the upper-class style but detest the mundane effort that yeasts into Prada, Yves St. Laurent, Versace and Armani. Where has my Rolls Royce gone? Long time passing. Mary has gone too. With the flowers that she made famous.

Wealth is yesterday. My literary legacy is tomorrow. I look forward to the glorification of my death. You can read about me. I have said it all. Talk to me. I will listen through dead, deaf ears.

It's not that I don't like money but I don't like the effort it takes to earn it. I'd rather write this poem. It goes to the soul. It invades the heart. Its value is not monetary.

Upside Downside

There is an upside and a downside,
An uptown and a downtown,
A west
And an east.

Call me an upper east side boy.
Boy?
I am seventy-four.
I am the presaged entertainment of death.
I was rich.
Now I am poor.
Rich man, Poor man.

The contrast is the percipient or the result
Of being bipolar.
I contrast.
I fly.
I dive.
I live.
I die.

I never read the book,
Rich Man, Poor Man.
I never saw the television show.
I am both.
And then some.
I am fabulous.
But if you want to know where I want to be,
It's on 74th Street,

Lighting up my life like our dining room chandelier.
Before the lights go out
As they will.
Not much left in my will.
I didn't save.

I won't be saved.
Words are coins.
I bank them.
I will face death like a gladiator.
I was born on the upper west side
But look forward to dying on Park Avenue.
Will limousines drive over my face?
I will be a sardine
In the pavement can of the road.
The horses on top of me will be wood.
I will brag that I once lived here.
But I won't be able to move my lips in the concrete.

Memoires Of *Le Cirque*

How do you feel when you were rich and now earn forty dollars
An hour teaching boxing?
I mean how do I feel?
I don't even know who I am.
I identify with the manners of the upper class
But am disgusted by their smirks
And their snoots
Pushing into the remainder of my pie.
Something about Will Smith and pie.
Will they play "Men In Black" at my poorly attended funeral.
I cry.
I dance.
It doesn't matter.
I dare to say to my wife,
"I just don't care."
I want to sneak out of my coop at three in morning
And chat with Park Avenue.
I want to say,
"I was once you, you were me and whatever we be
We weren't when we were all that jazz."
I am not really impressed by the superficial.
I hate riches.
But I would like to go back for one good meal to Le Cirque
Even though it is no longer there,
Nor is Serio,
And soon I will be a possible memory and I hope my wife sticks
Around a while after I have been carried like an empty dish

Back into the kitchen.
Live Lauren.
Die David.
Is that a coffin or pheasant under glass?

Biden's January 19th Speech

I am sitting in my room listening to Biden's speech. My room is commodious, not odious like Biden's intelligence. In truth he is speaking better than usual. Strong drugs, maybe. Perhaps amphetamines. Or like me he is taking donepezil. He thinks that God is a vaccine. He talks about the injection for the virus like it is a miracle, like walking on water, like resurrection. He thinks that he needs to poke his needle into the butt ends of our days. To Biden there is only one answer—camouflaged Alzheimer's. Give me your flat brain waves. I already have a bit of damage from boxing. Been knocked out a few times. I don't care. I hate to say that we are brain damaged brothers. You speak of science. Who are you kidding? You were a C student. What do you know about science? I was Phi Beta Kappa and I don't know shIt about science. I don't want to. It bores me. It is glorified mechanics. I am a poet. I want to write your epitaph. I don't give a sh.t about what is right or wrong but you are wrong for America and we should cabinet the spaces in your brain. I open the refrigerator door. You have taken out all the ice and pretend you are friendliness of the warm stove. There is nothing lower than a president except you. I would like to step on you like a cockroach. Hey Jay, there are alien bugs in this world. "Men in Black" again. Biden is letting them all in through the southern border. He is a rich man on a politician's meagre salary. He can afford to buy a black suit and pretend that he is a movie star when he can't memorize the lines that he read from the teleprompter.

Ruff, Ruff

When I was upper east side, I was a snowflake, a doyly,
A table setting in a castle,
Limoges
Or better —Florian Pape?
The Pope's dishes,
which my wife sold
For fifteen thousand dollars to a rich Honduran woman.

I am panting after your silk negligee,
Ruff, ruff.
Married fifty years to Lauren and she still sparkles
Like a moment's breath or a flirtation.
I was caviar scooped with a soup spoon out of a jar.
I was all that and then some.

Now I am an ex-con.
A parttime boxing coach for twenty years.
I am shit.
But I feel relieved to not lift my leg up at society's curb
And piss all over my shoes.

Can you imagine working twelve hours a day in a boring
Office just so that you can pat yourself on the back
And say, "You did good?"
I don't want to wear designer labels,
Cartier watches
Or live in a staid coop.
But I do.

I mean I once was part of that world and the world

Had me in its way and gave me
Goodies like my life
Was Christmas.
Thank you.
You're welcome.
I don't care.
But I do.
I am thankful for what I did but I am happy to still live
Off what I have done even though I no longer have to do it.
Ruff, ruff,
I love you like a dog and want you to pat my neck
And nuzzle my nose.
I still live in the upper east side even though the upper
East side doesn't live in me.
What I really like to do is write and fight.

I have published fifteen books.
I have sparred ten thousand rounds, fought six professional fights,
Nine amateur fights and seventy white collar bouts.
A few professional exhibitions.
That is me.

I am not the weak, niggling, petty men on the upper east side.
I am the glorification of a tough rose.
I am what any man would like to tend in his garden.
Well, the brain damage?
It gives me the creative joint.

Living With Imaginary Cockroaches

Location is not vocation so I am living on the rich upper east side
But I am the life squeezed out of an orange
A date with a squashed grape where I am the poor rind
Of an avocado.
Test me,
Love me,
Rankle me with your sweet introspective lips.

What has happened to you Kaye?
That's from *Men in Black*,
I think.
I am not where I live but live where I am not
In the lower classes with the absent cockroaches horrifying
My wife and making intelligence a fallen thought.
I am back.
I am not black.

I am a white man who was stupid enough to lose all his assets.
It light firecrackers in my socks to feel what it's like
To walk without the support of ankles.

Was It All Worth It?

It's not that I am a crybaby baby but that what I lost is more than what you all had and I am standing testimony to my refusal to let sadness seep out of my business failure. Bad is good. So what, I lived on the upper east side. I still live there. I am commodious with the commode and threaded with my Persian rug. My mirror is eighteenth century. Everyone who lived then is dead. Was it all worth it? I look forward to my extermination. This life is a raw deal. To thank God is to defy logic and accept the horror of the shortness of our space. I see myself in a plastic tub swashing around the Atlantic Ocean. Where do I go? Where do I come from? Was all this worth it? It was. It is. I am starry eyed even though the stars died or are in the process of it. Will the upper east side live after me? Of course. Everything will. My balls are squeezed by a metal nutcracker. I eat myself up. Pass the salt. My tongue swells. The lighthouse in Montauk sheds no light on the bipolar waves.

Ex-Con

I was glorious.
I was doilies.
I was a table setting in a castle.
I was porcelain dishes.
I was the panting that followed your silk nighty.
I was all that and then some.
Now I am an ex-con.
The seasons change.
Fate falls upon itself like autumn leaves.
I was rich.
I still am—emotionally.
A boxing coach for twenty years.
No tears.
It is a lowly profession.
I reject other opinions and the snobbery
Of the stupid elite.
I drum to a different beat.
Boxing is still fun.
I publish my joys like a mop
Of hip hop shining the quotidian floors.
I've done a lot of things.
I am diverse.
Things have done a lot to me and I took the punches
Never crying about the brain damage.
Call me brave.
That is a coward's point of view.

My Fair Lady

I am on the F train leaving York Street.
Shame, rhyme, oh my.
Why aren't I we on the upper east side?
Thank the God of transportation—
The MTA
I will soon be uptown.
I am on my way.
I love the upper east side.
I love you my Fair Lady, Lauren,
You are class.
I am telling the rich truth heading to Park Avenue
On the loose I am exploring the value of nostalgia.
Love has nothing to do with designations
Or subway stops.
It the suspension of judgments in God's glass of water.

Early

It is Saturday at 6:30 AM and I am walking down Park Avenue to go to the F train to York Avenue in Brooklyn. Gleason's Gym don't go away; come and stay on this freezing day. The icy upper east side is quiet like an oyster, fresh meat of introspection between the shells. I remember how my grandfather, Max, used to open the oysters with a knife. He caught them in his backyard on Lake Montauk. I open the wonders of the neighborhood with eyes-closed observation. I am worried that I will become an early morning casualty. Crime is rampant. Felons are in collusion with the morticians. It is all about money. Or that is the excuse for blood lust. My body is small change among the frequent murders. De Blasio is the red cape that the murders are charging after at like bulls with bullshit excuses. Somehow murder is out of joint with the proper upper east side. We or they are too rich to die. Last night on the news I saw that a 22-year-old cop was shot dead in Harlem. Uptown is another country. For me the upper east side ends in the eighties. Dangerous is as dangerous does. The politicians blame it on the guns. What about the woman pushed onto the subway tracks and the one stabbed by a homeless man. Does dangerous do in my neighborhood? No. On occasion. Yes. It all doesn't matter. I am 76. One day I will be no one's memory of the city. Time gives and gets the death penalty.

The Miracles

I am at Gleason's Gym in Brooklyn. My parents were born in Brooklyn. It always sounded like a slum to me. It is not. But then again it is not the upper east side where dreams are the casual awakenings of birds in dead wood trees and life is something that subsided from life and is the death of fabulous prewar buildings. I like Dumbo. I love New York. I love myself. I hate myself. I am the subway that goes beneath my smile and finds meaning in the "tracks of my tears." That's song was by Smokey Robinson. How does he look so young at his age? He is a miracle. Perhaps I am from the Miracles. I look pretty good for 76 and am physically fit as a 30-year-old. I am the subway that goes beneath my smile and finds meaning in the tracks of my tears. I am the life of my party. I never lost my girl. I love my girl. Lauren is my world. Even when she is disagreeable. But I lost myself. I can't find me. Tonight I will hide beneath the couch in my living room. I don't want the coop board to see that I can't pay their phony assessment. I don't want them to see that "my smile looks out of place."

To Die on The Upper East Side

I was born on the upper west side. Slum. A bum of an experience. Oh,,oh,oh, now it has become classy, nouveau riche, a bitch to deal with like a spoiled girl. Now don't tell me about spoiled men. That's not my province. I don't believe in women's lib. I believe in male liberation from the lure of female beauty. Women are treats. But women are treated. Their hands are filled before they are out. What is given takes. They are fakes that gather real rewards. What the hell. What I wanted to say was that I lived most of my life on the upper east side and want to die most of my death there. The real estate values are more sincerely better. They are not nouveau and meretricious. I want to lie amongst the rich soil and have my skull polished by classy doormen at 749 Park Avenue.

Going Home Big Mama

Big mama has nothing to do with my trip home.
I am tripping.
I am manic.
Not in a panic but happy as a constant digression.
Remember that song by Roxanne Shante,
"Save all the drama
Cause here comes the Big Mama."
Remember that song?
I don't.

I get on the F train at York Street.
Redundancy is not lack of imagination but repetitive joy
Is my perspective's persuasion.
Do I want to hang myself from a silk stocking,
Poke out my eyes
Or jump down onto the train tracks?
Neither. None. Anon like that old Shakespearean rag.
Eliot levels it.
I am the canon of literature.
I studied a lot when I was young.
That is my Ph.D.,
Not yours.
So if you criticize me, you show off your ignorance.

I want to live; I want to frolic.
No, I don't because my disposition
Is often colic.
Fun is only fun to the simple-minded.
A laugh is a lack of introspection,

A mouthful of hay,
Hey, hey, hey.

I don't know what I want.
I am not wanting.
I am stuffed with my own personal traits
Like a pillow with feathers under my own
Predisposed head.

I hope I don't kill myself.
I'm afraid I don't have the control to resist
The impulsion of the thought.
I am dominated by my fear
Of lack of control when I back myself up
Like a drumroll.
"No I am not Prince Hamlet nor was meant to be,"
But I am.
I am a suicide.
I am Hemingway.
I am Sylvia Plath.
I am "Almost at times the Fool."

But I will not kill myself.
It is an intrusive thought, an obsession that
Obsession is intellect instead of weakness.

I shall grow old.
I will not die next to Hamlet.
I shall wear the bottoms of my trousers rolled.

When I get out at 63rd Street and Lexington Avenue I shall
Wear designer jeans and walk like a peach
Of upper-class society

When in actuality I am the pear that has fallen from a bag
Onto the street.

I am probably the only person on 74th Street that has done
Jail time.

You don't do life for tax evasion.
I have done life in my life where I am imprisoned in mood swings
As permanent as bars.

All the people inside of me line up for commissary where
We can buy candies, popcorn
And watches.

The homeless call jail their home and look for fights
To get extra time.

The vagrants like three square meals and a cot.
Compared to the streets that's a lot.
It's not not.
It's a place to come home to when they never leave.

I am a poet criminal.
Like Prufrock I have "heard the mermaids singing each to each."

The Roulette Wheel Spins

When my finances go south the upper east side follows it
And death is a sour ball that breaks my teeth.
Last year my dentist cost me ten thousand dollars.
I have a denture for my front tooth.
When I take it out,
I look like the homeless.
Sadness is irreconcilable with the rich smiles
Of my uptown neighbors.
They curl themselves into balls and bounce
Up the monied stairs
Like Spalding's of ambition.
I hate earning money.
It is like stuffing my head in a bag and breathing the constrictions
Of the menial world.
This morning I walked over to Citibank to deposit
$120 in my checking account so that my check to Spectrum
Wouldn't bounce like an absent
Spalding.
When I moved to the upper east side, I was rich like a bitch.
Now I am hanging on like a molar that needs root canal.
My fortune has gone south.
I'd like to move to a cheap house in Del Ray Florida.
Like the one my father lived in when I ruined his business
And after his wife died.
I guess it's my turn next.
The roulette wheel spins and no one ever wins.
A temporary reprieve is the best you can do.
I buy myself a drink and attempt to ignore my emptying pockets.

Timber

I come and go as we all do when we don't have the footwork to take the next step and make tracks off of the planet. I want to stay. I want to see daylight and your smile. I want to be in style and not a corpse in a box. I don't want to die. Why? I don't know. I don't know much. I am impulses that are such and such. I am tomorrow's extension of today and the ratification of the vote for a dead candidate. My ears are in my hat so that they can't hear when they are warm. Every hundred years or so the world disappears. I disappear. I become not, a lot, and shot through with life's failure. I worry about the end but the end doesn't worry about me. Well, I don't really care. What happens happens and what doesn't happen is a reprieve, a broken watch. I've got something up my sleeve. I plan to live forever. My books will be the lever that lifts me above the grave. I am not grave. I am happy. I am my own legacy. If you don't agree, you will be dead too. I am hilarious. I mean, delirious. I can't make sense out of nonsense when my penchant is for death. If I eat a peach will I become a tree? Cut me down. Timber.

Dull Train

I am on the F train going to York Street in Brooklyn.
There is an alligator on the tracks.
No, there isn't.
It is in my bathtub when I was a boy and when then
Was when I was less than then.
All the unmerry people on the train look the same.
Not insane,
Dull,
Like their skulls have been lobotomized.

The coronavirus masks hide the nothing that is and was
And loquacious intellect is silent.
Where have all the smiles gone?
Long time masking.
The flowers have died.
The facial expressions are gone.

The absence of color is the lack of awareness of racism.
Grays, blacks, whites,
A fusion of lack of fashion in drab clothes.
Faces painted with oblique colors are washed out
Like the background atmosphere of motion.

There is no racism here.
There are no races.
Just gray shades of gray like Jimi Hendrix sang
Purple Haze all around
Don't know if I'm coming up or down.

I once took guitar lessons.
I insulted the strings.
I am not musical.
And you wouldn't want to hear me sing.

The train is a poor exhibition of failed volition
And sad travels within myself.
The drab passengers are lost in themselves
Like mice in a forest
Without cheese.

Going is gone and we are on the way to what
Is behind us
In the last cars.

Personality is drained from the faces that surround me.
Expressionless masks like smashed
Halloween disguises.
The upper class has died in the tunnel,
Expressionless.
I used to go to society parties.
Now I ride the F train.
The stench of failure is the longing for death.

Fred Astaire

I am hanging on to the ledge of my finances with fingernails that bleed in the air. I just don't care. But I do, ah, I do. I don't want to be poor. I want to dress in fanciness and lollygag around with the upper-class. I want to be the vest of the civilized and the momentum of the moment at a charity dinner. Let them starve. I want to die. No, no, no I want to be a teacup on a saucer in the hand of a delicate senior woman. I want to hear an absent harp play like the one before the coronavirus at the St. Regis Hotel. I am an uptown boy. I am not a boy. I am Fred Astaire on glass feet. I am charming. I am alarming when I trip over my own self-destructive thoughts. I won't be able to see if I blind myself. I close my closed eyes and erase the chalk from the lessons I drew on the blackboard. I put my cheek against the slate. Here I go again, I am "dancing cheek to cheek." School is out. I learn by not learning. I am deaf, dumb and blind. Somehow astute.

Black Bread

If I am suicidal, I will have to stab myself with a pearl handled knife because I am upper class and swell with the swell even though I have fallen from grace. I was in; now I am out of the chase, the race, wearing cotton instead of lace. I love you. I hate you. I am moody about myself and can't see what I see because I am the confusion in an apple and the core of insane pits. The pits. Life is tough. And yet I struggle and survive and learn to distance myself from myself and take it on the chin without losing my dimple. You look at me and wonder how I can stand myself. I don't. I lie down on the road and hope that a bus rides over me. Fill it with school children. Let them know the horror of roadkill and the shock uncontrollable thoughts. Be mental. I am. I am nuts. But I'm not, I tell you, I am not. I am the harp music in the St. Regis dining room. I am delicate. I am class. Tea sandwiches come in delicate pieces. I like them all. I want to put myself on the plate and eat my thoughts. It's nice to be nice. I spread etiquette on my black bread.

Rich Air

I want to live where I want to live because
It has become comfortable
And forty years
Is no drop in the bucket but a diamond
On a bracelet when you live on the Upper East Side.

I am surrounded by rich air
And I breathe in cotton candy and the little shrubs
In front of Ralph Lauren.

I know what I know.
Which is nothing.
I talk to myself like a butler
Whistling
While he polishes the chandeliers.

I almost live in a mansion.
Time is not as time was.
The bills elude me.
The ducks shit in the water.

I am distracted.
I am retracted from the world and the possibility of war
In the Ukraine.
I am too old to get drafted.
I don't have to get a psychiatrist's note
Like in Vietnam.

I am comfortable where I am comfortable
And don't want to move

To a location
That is visible and bangs against my elbows
Like a real location.

Spare me the real locus of the crocus.
My mom grew them in her garden and their name
Reminded me of death.
My parents are beneath the flower garden in the sky,
Bulbs,
Corpses,
The remains of nothing in a spade shoveling.

I go out this morning to buy a donut,
Coffee
And an egg.
It costs me five dollars,
I think.
I don't remember.
The past is slipping from me and I don't care.
I am the product of the future.
I am tomorrow's groceries on the shelves.

They say that D'Agostino's is no longer stocked.
They say that global warming lies beneath the frozen winter.
They say,
And get hysterical,
And are arrogant in their opinions.

You know what you know.
I don't know what you know.
Knowledge is for cripples who are hanging off a ledge
By painted fingernails.

At The Corner

When you live on the upper east side you don't pretend that you are down to earth because you are above the clouds over Central Park. I am not a regular guy. I am part of the part that is *high and mighty. I told my heart where to stop and start....* I know where. At the corner of 74th Street. This is my world. Cilla Black sang, "You're my world, you are my night and day/You're my world, you're every prayer I pray/ If our love ceases to be/Then it's the end of my world/End of my world/ End of my world for me." Wow. I love it. I love Lauren. I love 74th Street. It is my world. The end and the beginning. The substance. I never want to leave it. When I die I will steal the street sign and label heaven my corner. This could not happen in Soho. The upper east side is not Johnny come lately. It is the precursor of death, the stairway to Eric Clapton's heaven. Who will go first? His son did. But how about him or me?

My Place

My world is upside down. I live on the upside. The Upper East Side of New York where I am less than I am and more than you are and something that is nothing if nothing is something to brag about. I am me and you are you. I am the traffic light. I am the hydrant. I am the bum sleeping in Eve St. Laurent's doorway. I hate the homeless. I always feel sorry for what I hate because what I hate is what I love even though the stench is annoying. When I was rich I used to give the bums money. Now I want to kick them in the head for reminding me of my many failures. Life is a step off the curb where you break your ankle. I have broken mine. But I still hop and skip because mania is an attitude not a conclusion. It is beautiful. I am beautiful for a 75-year-old ex-con. I used to model. Well, real people modeling. I was the subway bum poster. I still have a head of hair. A slight bald spot maybe. A missing front tooth. I can handle it because self-love is blind. Do you mind? I am David.

Hansel And Gretel

Askance a lane of literary verbiage pierces
My upper east side lip.
Give me lip.
Mine.

My heart is pricked by my financial losses.
I give my clients my arm
And substitute it with a bone.
Thin pickings.
But who is the witch and who is Hansel?
I trick them because they want to be tricked
And live in a hut in the middle
Of their hearts' woods.

My finger is a borrowed bone with which
I trick the witch
Who appears in the tale of Hansel and Gretel
And gets caught by the I.R.S.
And the slickness of good little children.
We take her diamonds.
A chocolate egg with gold is sweet.
Theft is just when someone is trying
To eat you.
We put her in a cage.
I did two years in a federal jail.

Cook the witch.
Afterall she is a bitch.

I starve.
I waste.
My tall tales are fake.
I am still not poor.
I have scattered assets.

Most poor people are fat.
I am not poor.
I am thin,
A junior welterweight.

I still have a few bucks under the rug.
So that's my life.
Maybe.
Shrug.

I go up and down even when I am uptown.
The clown in the trash
Is Joachim Phoenix joking about shooting
The walking dead.
His face is sickly sad.
He wears the makeup of self-hatred and grief.
I did a movie once,
"Boxer Rebellion."
It stank.
It was as sick as "The Joker."

I wore white face, not black face so you woke
Mother f..kers,
Don't accuse me.

My Neighborhood

Burglars are intimidated by the Upper East Side. They used to be scared of my Rolls Royce. They preferred to steal non-distinguishable Mercedes. They are frightened to mug in my neighborhood. They think there is a cop in every doorway, behind every tree, up the old ladies' skirts. My neighborhood, oh, my neighborhood is all starch, bleach and false eyelashes. I no longer belong here. I am the residue of a bad prison sentence for something I really didn't do but I wish I had because guilt suits me. I've gone down from wealth, health and money in a cough. My life is inside out. I relish uptown like a burger not cassoulet. I can afford a Big Mac and live where I live with money from yesterday. My life is a feast. I stalk my neighborhood and it rises like yeast in my estimation. It's all good. I do what I should and don't what I won't. I am uptown in a rainbow of riches raining on my destitute parade.

Redundant Travel

How many times must I get on the F train to not notice
That I am on it
And to erase the consciousness
Of redundant travel?

It should matter.
I am smothered with consciousness,
Flatted by my own self-interest.

Train, train, go away
Come again another day.

I am on my way to Brooklyn.
Gleason's Gym is my borough.
I am Sancho Penza
Riding a donkey,
Dapple.

I am a joke.
It is not funny that I lost all my money
And don't care.

Leave me alone.
I am dispersion in the wing.

I am the mania of an excuse
Of false confidence
Of a boast to a bully whom I could never beat.

That's a Classy Name

It is a cold wind that blows on January 27th. A date that will live in infamy. No, that was FDR's line. This day will live in khaki like I did on visiting days in jail. I live on Park Avenue. That's a classy name. It's a shame that I am no longer rich. The cold air is an ice pop, a delicious flavor, a breath of detoxicated spice and everything nice. I can't wait to get to my neighborhood and out of the subterranean tunnel air of the subway. I hope my lungs freeze into ice cubes. I want to die in a glacial shower and open the shower curtains and show myself to myself in the naked mirror. I am not an exhibitionist. I am just trying to find myself by looking. Let me be the naked day in the stuttering lexicon of a man who says that he is handsome whether or not anyone else sees it.

Biography:

I have been in almost every magazine or newspaper in the world. Not always because of my writing. Mostly because of my boxing. Some of the papers that have written about me are—People Magazine, New York Times, Newsday (twice), Post (four times),Sports Illustrated, American Health (cover), C.F.O., Crain's (twice), New York Magazine, Signature, Ring Magazine, The Sun, Men's Journal, Source Magazine, Pursuits, London Mirror, Brutus (Japan),Time Out (New York and England) Coupe (France), Quick (Germany), Sport (Germany), Stern (Germany), Globe and Mirror(Canada), You (London), Star (London), The Brooklyn Eagle, and The Adirondack Review.

Some of the books I have written are— Living on Madison Avenue(Future Cycle Press) , Lane Changes (Four Way Books), Dementia Pugilistica (Mudfish), Steel Toe Boots (Fithian Press), Blame It On The Scientists (Pudding House Publications), King of White Collar Boxing (Rain Mountain Press), Broken Paragraphs (Black Spring Pub.. UK). Also Cyberwit published, This Book About Nothing, Coronavirus Breaks the Back of New York, The Interrupted Sky, A Cup of Crazy, God is Me. Whoopee and Beaten Up by Poetry. Invading God's Possible Universe (Wipf and Strompf.) Nuts!! How I finally Cracked the Shell: The Bipolar 21 Day Misadventures of a Former Wall Street CEO is a memoir being published by The University of West Alabama Press. The Suicide of Embers (Tebot Bach.)

TELEVISION: The Phil Donahue Show, George Michael's Sports Machine, NBC, BBC Good Sport, CBS 48 Hours, ABC Business World, CNN, MSNBC, Eyewitness News, MSG, MSNBC, CNN, ESPN, USA Network Fights, CTV (Canadian television); German, Chinese, Japanese, Spanish and Italian television.

I was a rapper and had three charted albums, "The Renegade Jew," "Da Masta Plan" and "Lifestyles." I wrote the lyrics for Sam Wayman's "Magic Man" on Polygram Records. I was a professional boxer and started the current rage in white collar boxing.

I wrote, produced and starred in "Boxer Rebellion" which was a feature film that played at the Sundance Film Festival. Also, I have a Ph.D. in literature and published a thousand poems and articles that appeared in periodicals.

www.ingramcontent.com/pod-product-compliance
Lightning Source LLC
LaVergne TN
LVHW040910150826
845672LV00007B/1976

* 9 7 8 8 1 1 9 2 2 8 6 3 8 *